Sugar Skulls Coloring Book

Adult Color By Numbers Coloring Book

BLACK BACKGROUND

Day of the Dead - Dia De Los Muertos

BY COLOR QUESTOPIA

Copyright © 2021

All rights reserved. No part of this publication may be reproduced, distributed, or transmitted in any form or by any means, including photocopying, recording, or other electronic or mechanical methods, without the prior written permission of the publisher

Our Color Palette Tips

1. **Colors corresponding to each number are shown on the back cover of the book - NEW- There are only 25 colors total in this book, with one "Flesh Tone" color where you can choose any flesh tone!**

   Each number corresponds to a color shown on the back of the book. **There will sometimes be an asterisk (*) that corresponds to "Any Flesh Tone."**

   To the left of each image, there's a list of colors used within that particular image. Simply match the numbers on the images to the colors on the list. If you tear a page out of the book, you can simply use the color key on the back of the book to match your colors. If you don't have an exact color match, that's totally fine. Feel free to use a similar color or shade. Although this is a color by number book, it's completely okay to get creative and change up the colors listed. You can let your imagination run wild, and color the images with whichever colors you like and have. The numbers are here to be a guide and to allow you to color without having to focus your energy on choosing colors.

2. **If there are any spaces on an image without a number, you can go ahead and leave that space white (blank)**

   You can leave any space without a number white (blank), or you can fill that space in with any color you like. Another idea is to color that space in with a white color (for example, if you'd like to use a shiny white or a different shade of white on an image.)

3. **Bonus Images may have a slightly different color palette**

   Because the bonus images are from previous books with slightly different color palettes, they may include colors that aren't on the back of this book. Simply match them the best that you can, or choose completely different colors if you like. You are the artist and you are allowed to relax and enjoy!

Color By Number Tips

1. Relax and have fun

Let your cares slip away as you color the images. Take your time. Coloring is a meditative activity and there's no wrong way to do it. Feel free to color as you listen to music, watch TV, lounge in bed- do whatever relaxes you most! You can also color while you're out and about- on the train or at a cafe- take the book with you anywhere you go. Coloring is therapeutic and is great for stress relief and relaxation!

2. Choose your coloring tools

Everyone has their favorite coloring markers, crayons, pencils, pens- even paints! Feel free to color with any tool that you like! If you choose markers or paints, we recommend putting a blank sheet of paper or cardboard behind each image, so that your colors don't run onto the next image.

3. Test out your colors

Feel free to test out your colors on our Color Test Sheet, and use our Custom Color Chart to make the color choices your own!

Relax and Enjoy!

1. Black

4. Brown

5. Dark Brown

6. Tan

8. Red

10. Orange

12. Yellow

15. Green

17. Aqua Green

21. Lilac

24. Vivid Pink

1. Black

4. Brown

6. Tan

8. Red

9. Orange Red

12. Yellow

15. Green

17. Aqua Green

18. Light Blue

19. Blue

21. Lilac

22. Violet

23. Pink

24. Vivid Pink

1. Black

6. Tan

8. Red

9. Orange Red

10. Orange

12. Yellow

15. Green

17. Aqua Green

18. Light Blue

20. Dark Blue

21. Lilac

23. Pink

24. Vivid Pink

1. Black

6. Tan

8. Red

10. Orange

12. Yellow

15. Green

16. Dark Green

17. Aqua Green

19. Blue

20. Dark Blue

21. Lilac

23. Pink

24. Vivid Pink

1. Black

5. Dark Brown

6. Tan

8. Red

10. Orange

12. Yellow

16. Dark Green

17. Aqua Green

20. Dark Blue

24. Vivid Pink

1. Black

4. Brown

6. Tan

8. Red

10. Orange

12. Yellow

15. Green

16. Dark Green

19. Blue

20. Dark Blue

21. Lilac

22. Violet

24. Vivid Pink

5. Dark Brown

8. Red

9. Orange Red

10. Orange

12. Yellow

14. Light Green

15. Green

16. Dark Green

17. Aqua Green

19. Blue

20. Dark Blue

21. Lilac

22. Violet

*. Any Flesh Tone

1. Black
4. Brown
6. Tan
7. Peach
8. Red
9. Orange Red
10. Orange
12. Yellow
15. Green
17. Aqua Green
19. Blue
20. Dark Blue
21. Lilac
23. Pink
24. Vivid Pink

1. Black

8. Red

9. Orange Red

10. Orange

12. Yellow

15. Green

16. Dark Green

18. Light Blue

20. Dark Blue

21. Lilac

23. Pink

24. Vivid Pink

*. Any Flesh Tone

1. Black

5. Dark Brown

8. Red

10. Orange

12. Yellow

15. Green

17. Aqua Green

22. Violet

24. Vivid Pink

1. Black

6. Tan

7. Peach

8. Red

12. Yellow

14. Light Green

15. Green

16. Dark Green

17. Aqua Green

18. Light Blue

22. Violet

23. Pink

24. Vivid Pink

1. Black
6. Tan
8. Red
9. Orange Red
10. Orange
12. Yellow
13. Golden Yellow
15. Green
16. Dark Green
17. Aqua Green
21. Lilac
22. Violet
23. Pink
24. Vivid Pink

1. Black

5. Dark Brown

6. Tan

8. Red

10. Orange

11. Light Yellow

12. Yellow

15. Green

17. Aqua Green

19. Blue

22. Violet

24. Vivid Pink

1. Black

2. Gray

3. Dark Gray

5. Dark Brown

6. Tan

7. Peach

9. Orange Red

10. Orange

12. Yellow

14. Light Green

15. Green

16. Dark Green

22. Violet

23. Pink

24. Vivid Pink

1. Black

4. Brown

5. Dark Brown

6. Tan

7. Peach

8. Red

10. Orange

12. Yellow

17. Aqua Green

18. Light Blue

19. Blue

20. Dark Blue

21. Lilac

22. Violet

23. Pink

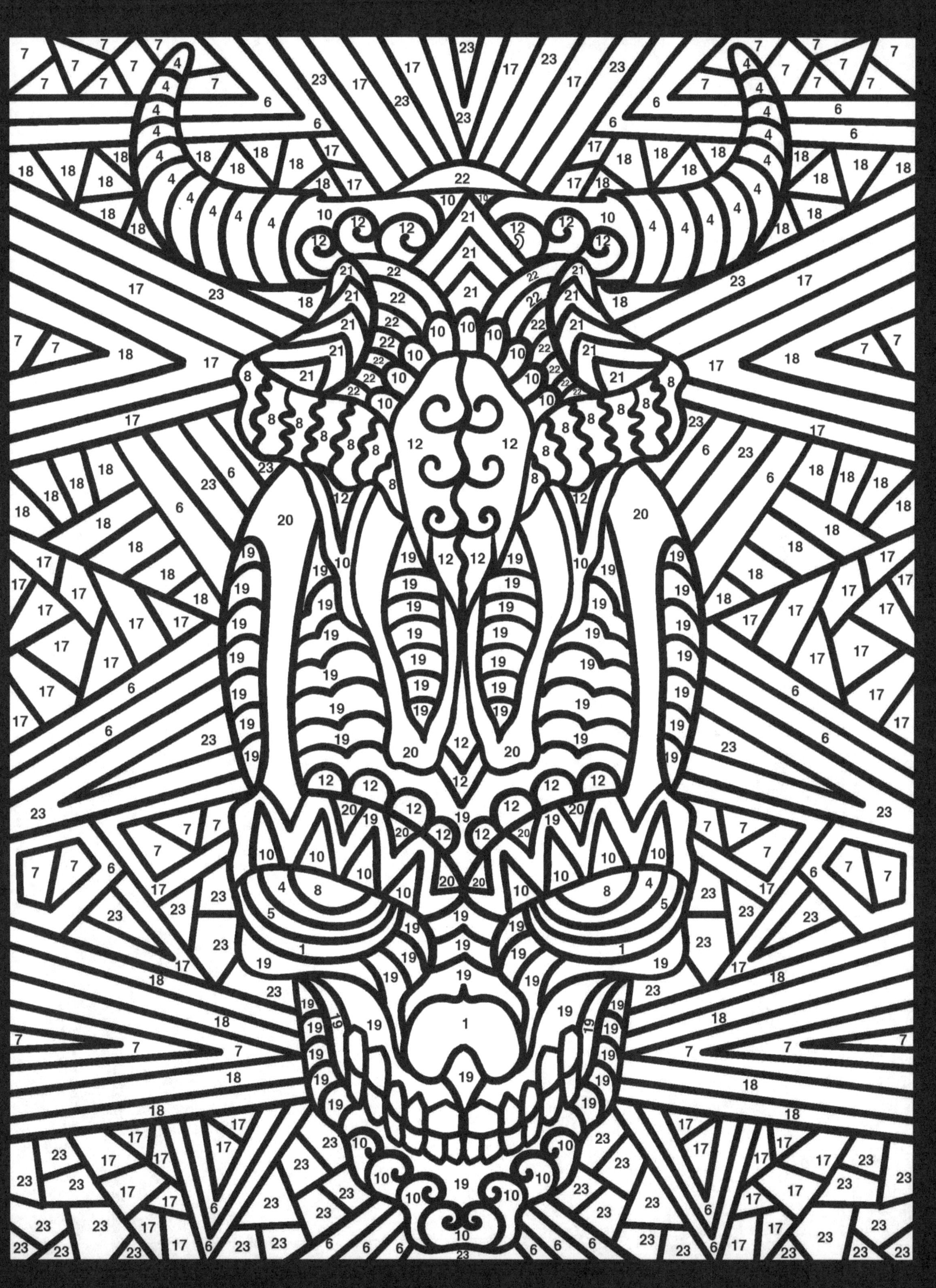

1. Black

4. Brown

5. Dark Brown

6. Tan

8. Red

12. Yellow

17. Aqua Green

19. Blue

21. Lilac

*. Any Flesh Tone

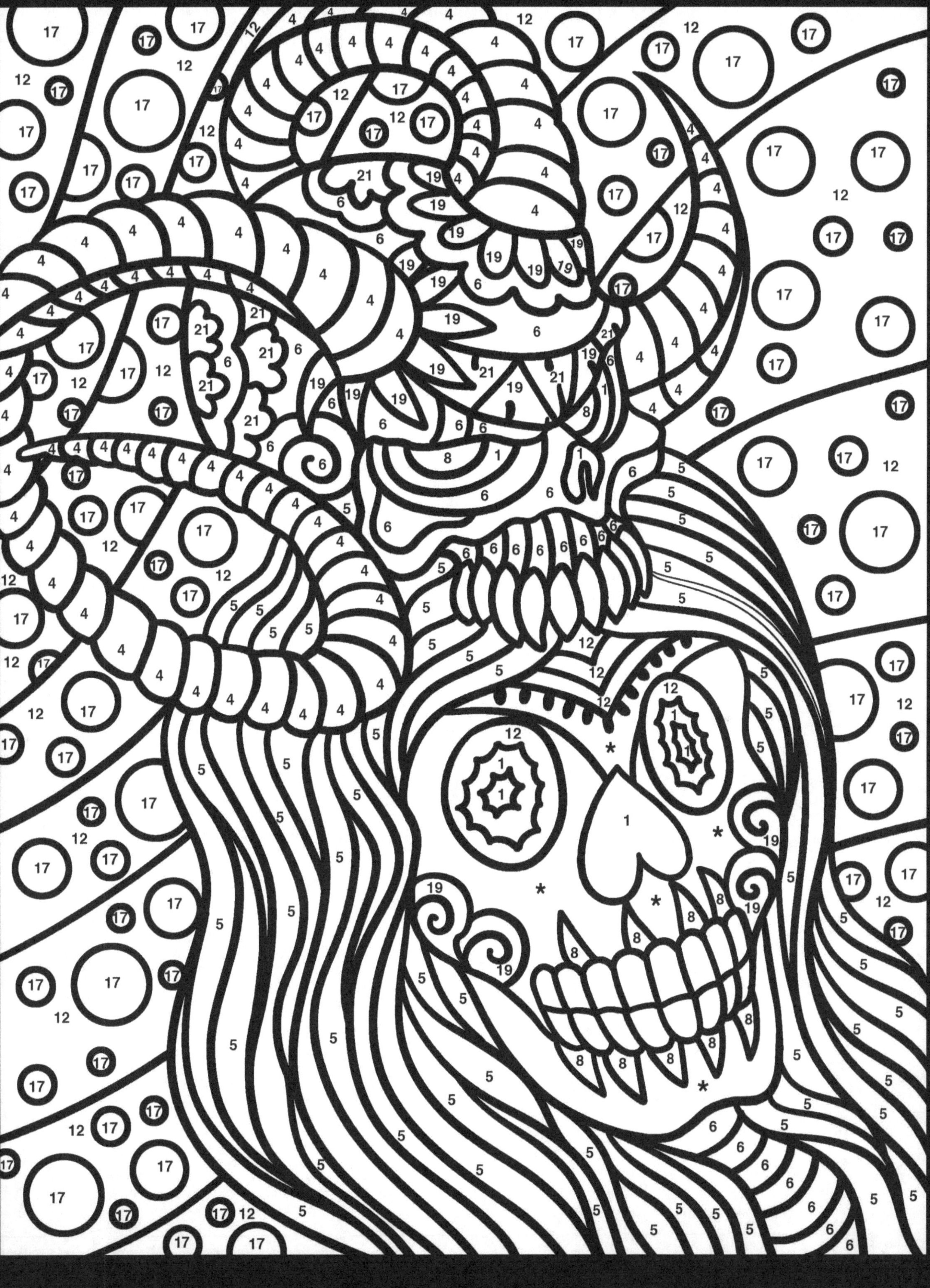

5. Dark Brown

6. Tan

10. Orange

11. Light Yellow

14. Light Green

20. Dark Blue

22. Violet

23. Pink

24. Vivid Pink

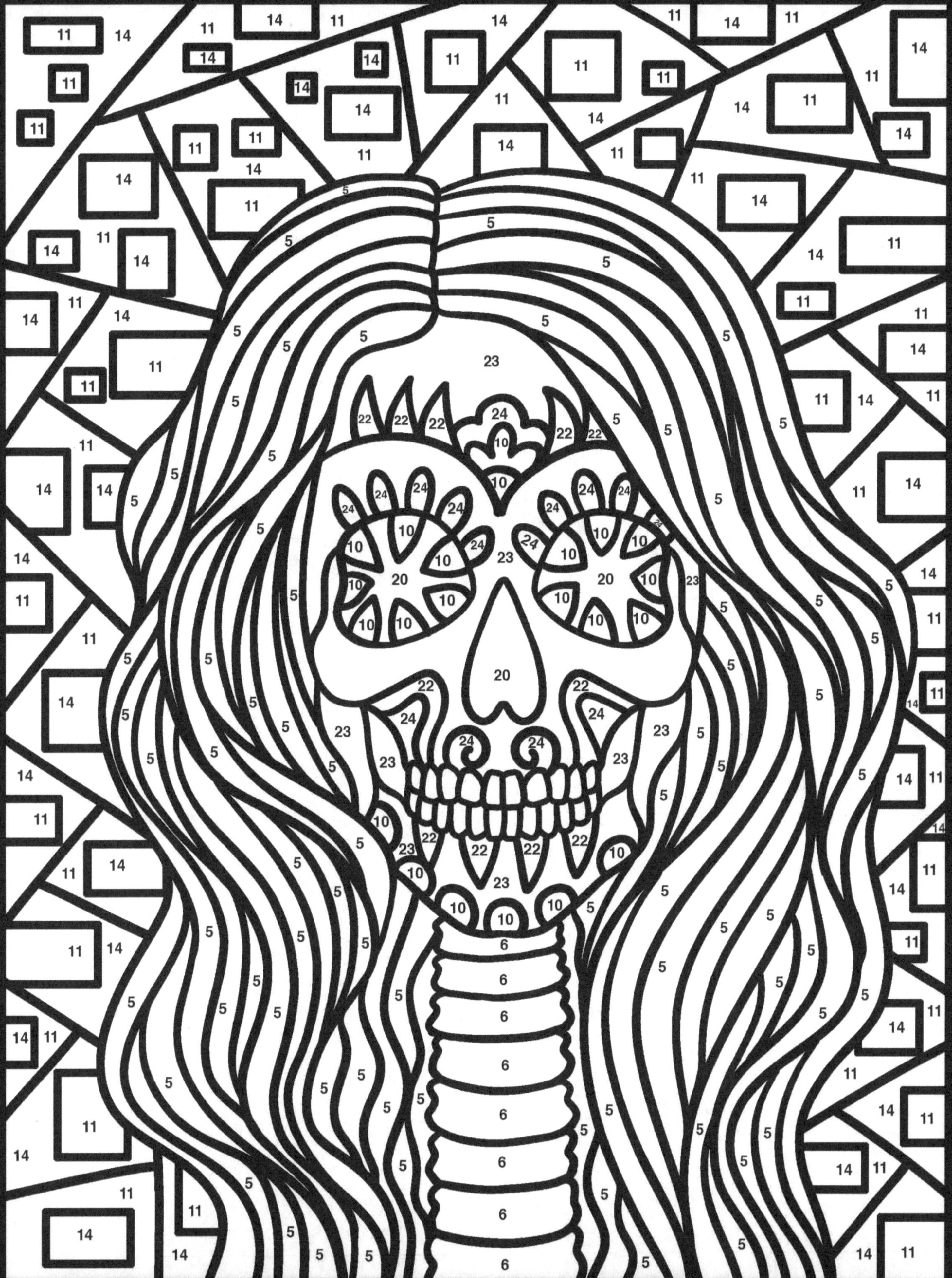

1. Black
4. Brown
7. Peach
8. Red
10. Orange
13. Golden Yellow
15. Green
16. Dark Green
17. Aqua Green
18. Light Blue
20. Dark Blue
21. Lilac
22. Violet
24. Vivid Pink

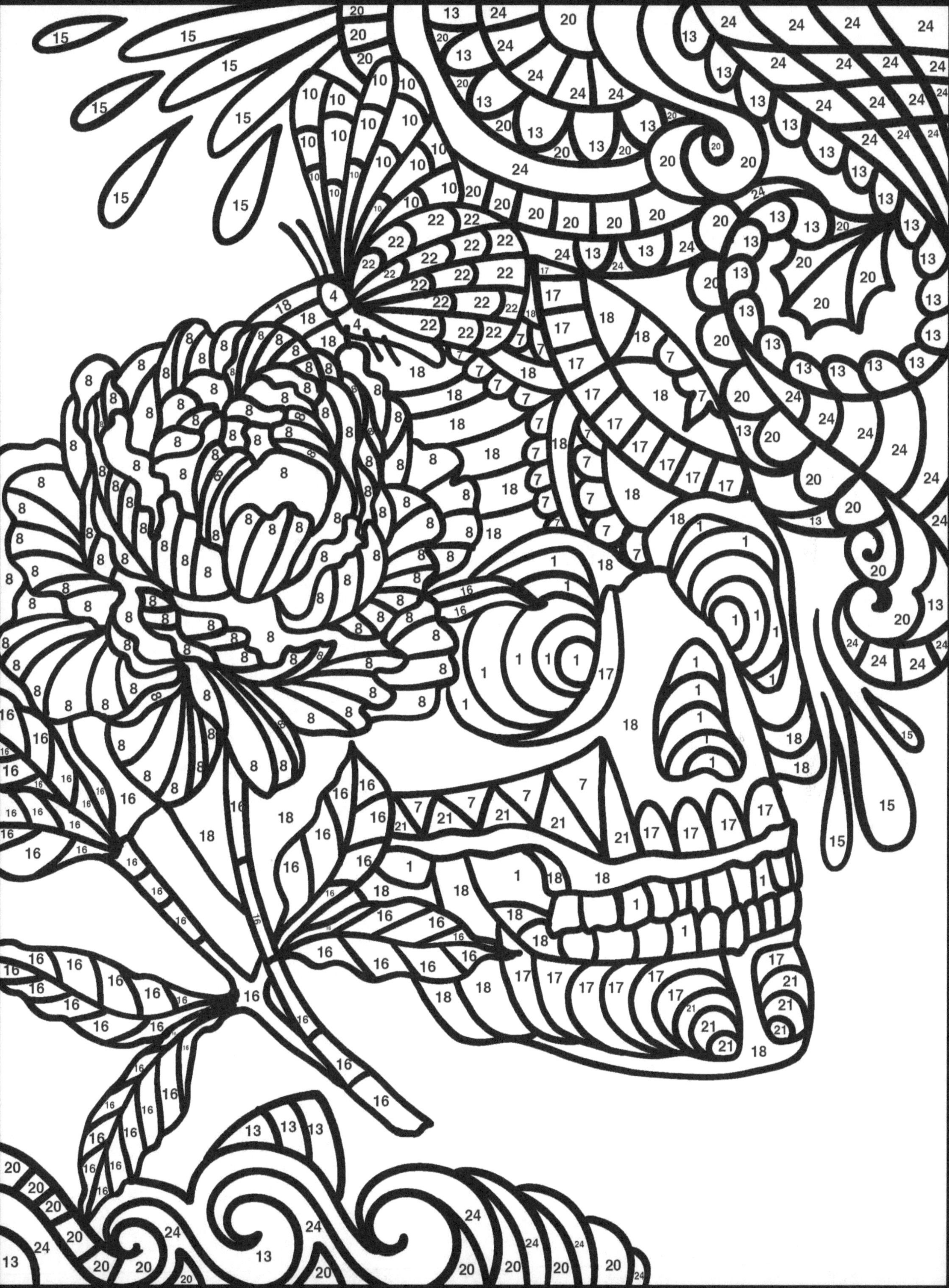

1. Black
5. Dark Brown
6. Tan
7. Peach
8. Red
9. Orange Red
10. Orange
11. Light Yellow
12. Yellow
15. Green
17. Aqua Green
20. Dark Blue
21. Lilac
22. Violet
23. Pink
24. Vivid Pink

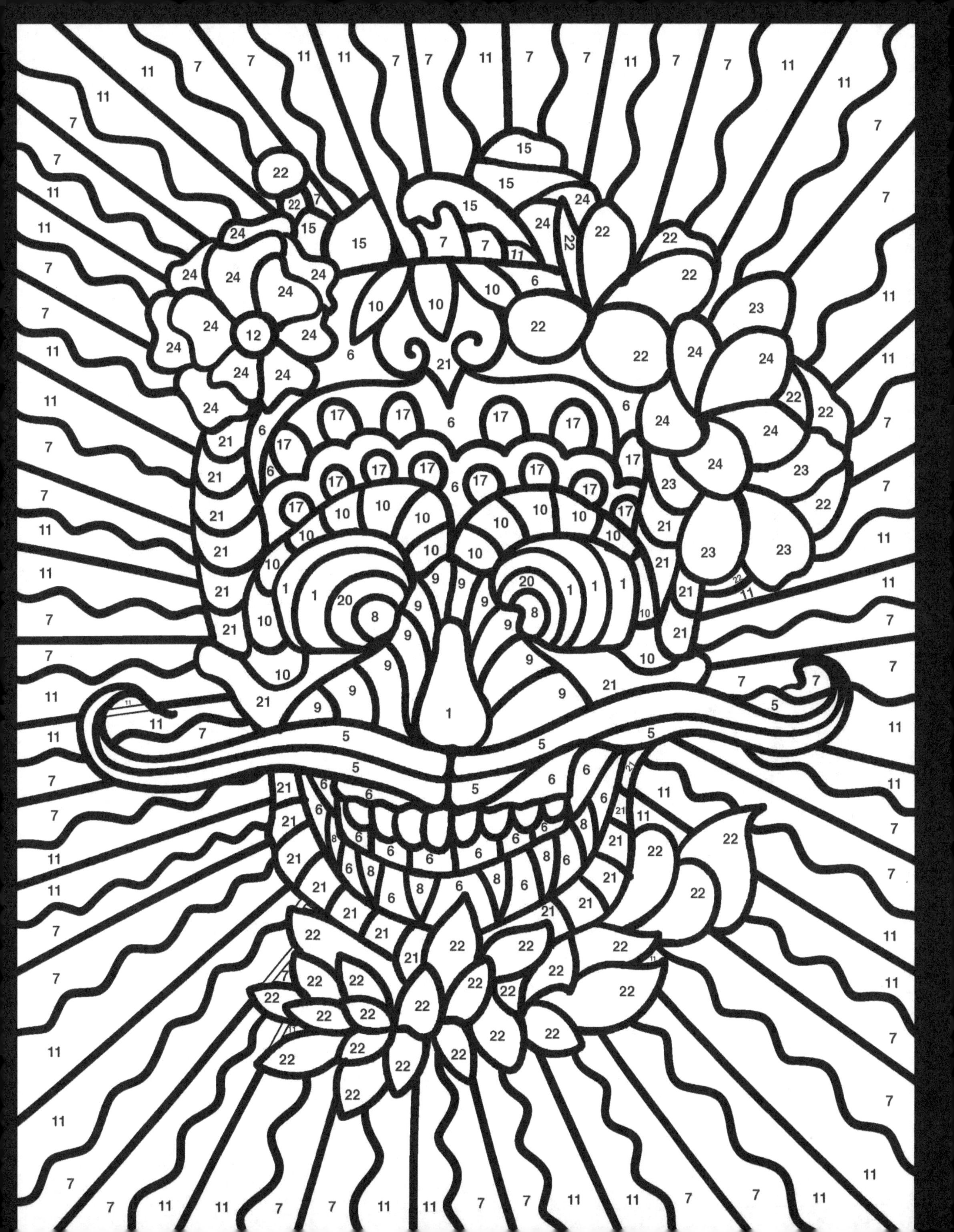

1. Black

4. Brown

5. Dark Brown

6. Tan

8. Red

10. Orange

12. Yellow

13. Golden Yellow

17. Aqua Green

18. Light Blue

19. Blue

22. Lilac

✱ . Any Flesh Tone

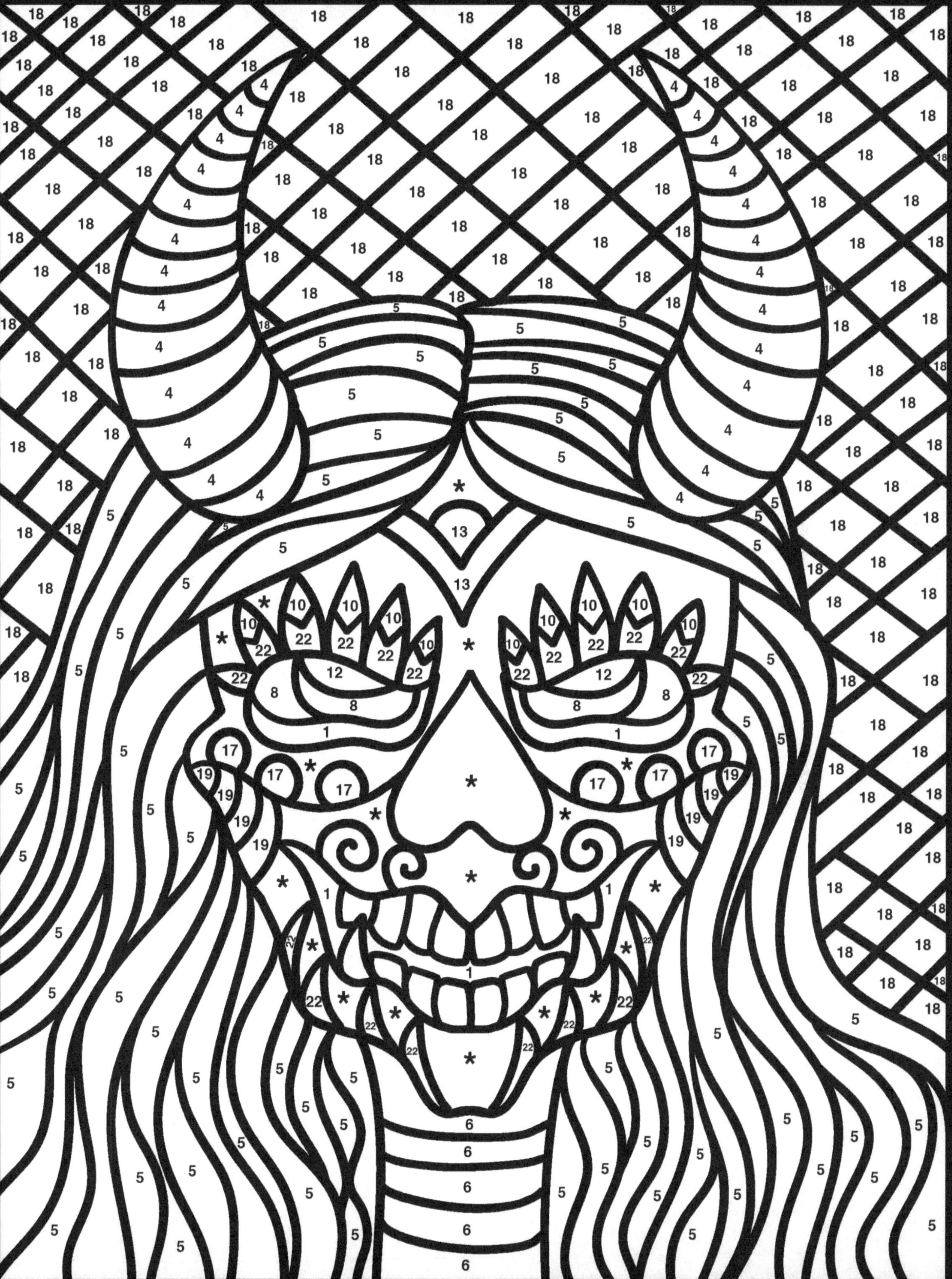

Enjoy Bonus Images From Some of Our Other Fun Color By Number Books!

Find All of Our Books on Amazon

HALLOWEEN
BLACK BACKGROUND
Scary Mosaic Fantasy Adult Color By Number

1. Neon Green
2. Light Green
3. Green
4. Beige
5. Black
6. Light Brown
7. Brown
8. Orange
9. Pink
10. Yellow
11. Violet
12. Purple
13. Light Violet
14. Red
15. Light Yellow

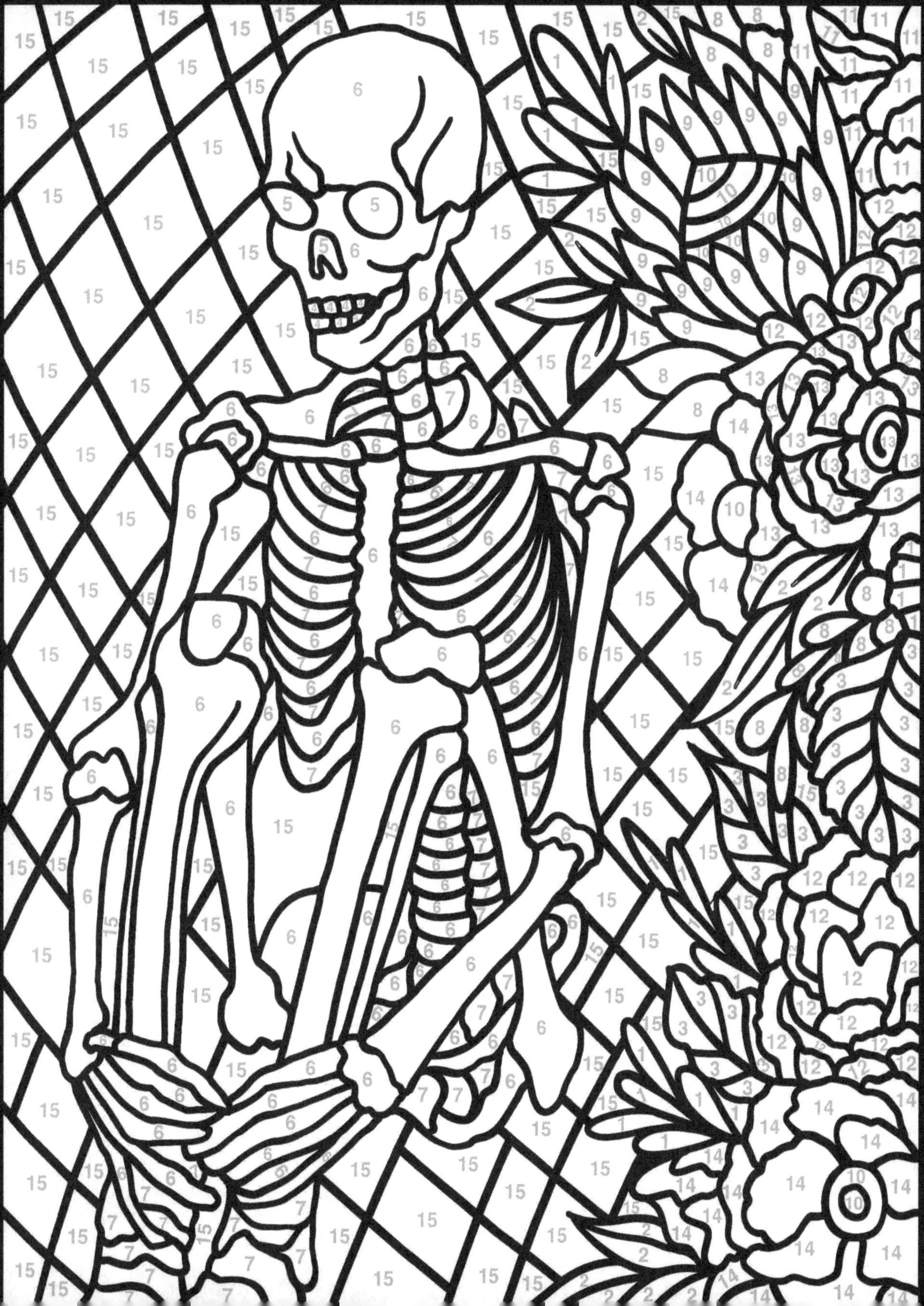

Horror and Nightmare Creatures
BLACK BACKGROUND
Mosaic Color By Number

1. Black
2. Dark Gray
3. Medium Gray
4. Gray
5. Red
6. Dark Red
7. Dark Brown
8. Beige
9. Brown
10. Army Green
11. Navy Blue
12. Dark Violet
13. Dark Blue

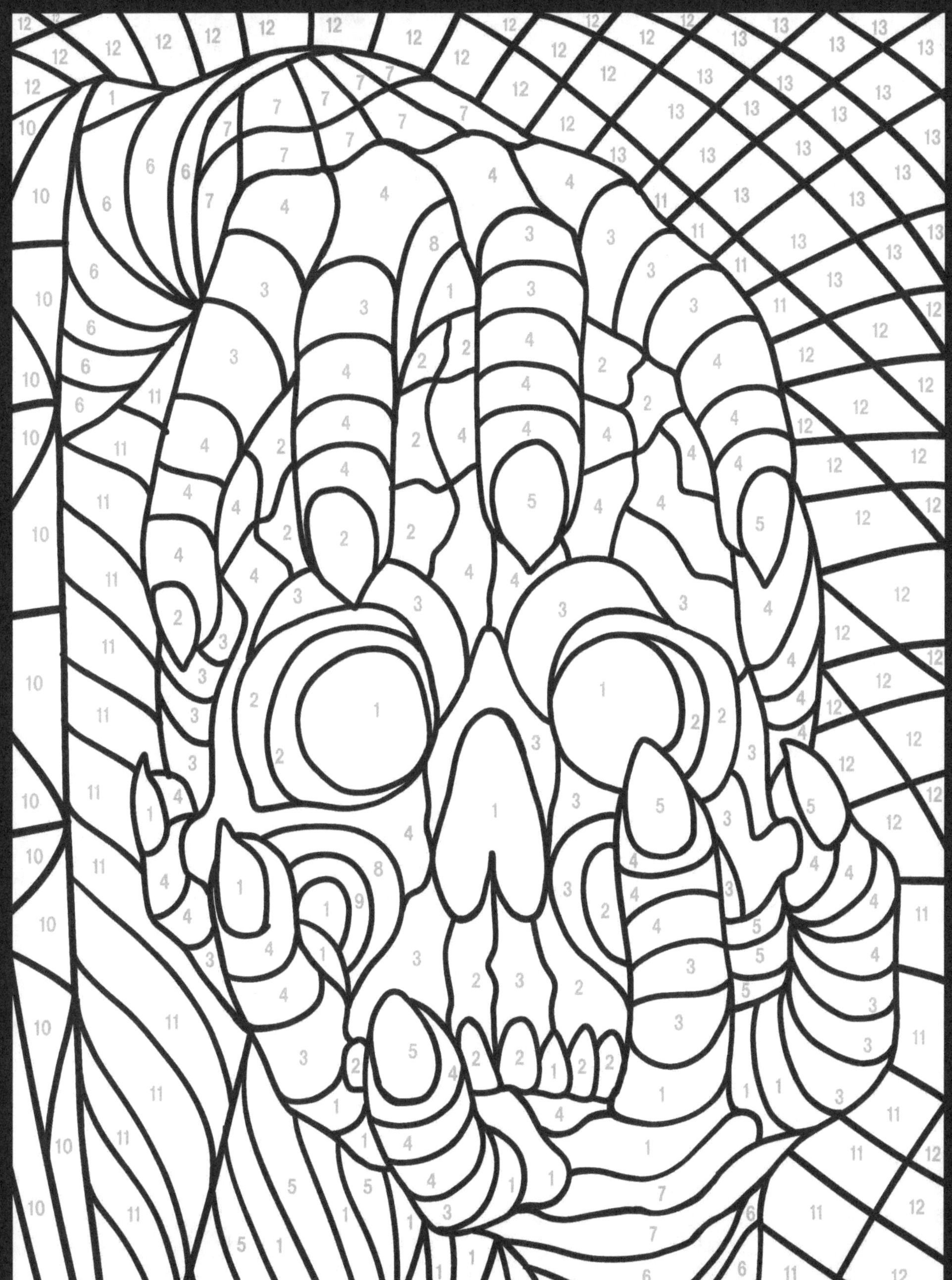

SPACE COLORING BOOK
BLACK BACKGROUND
GALAXY COLOR BY NUMBER
FOR ADULTS AND KIDS
OF ALL AGES

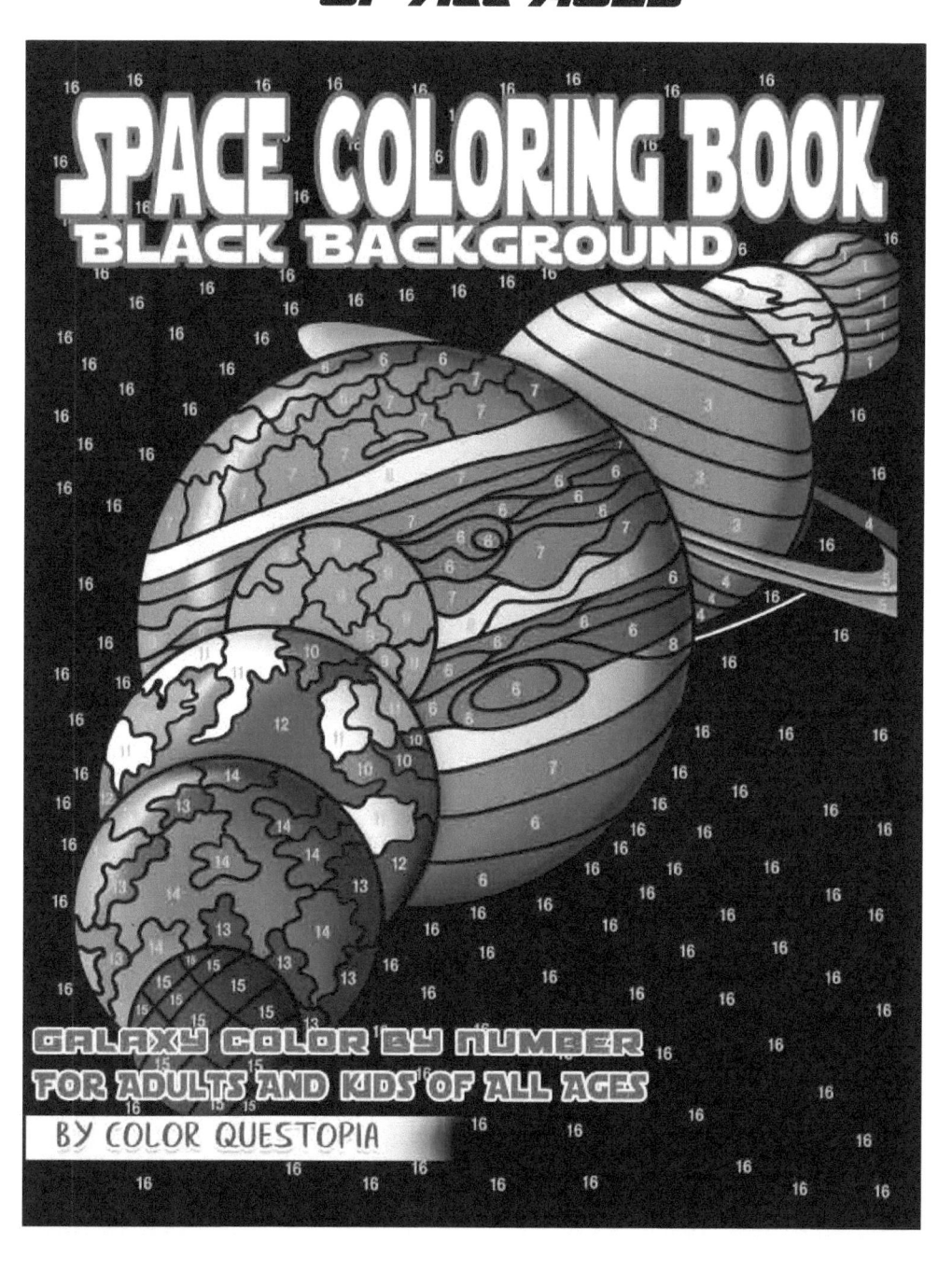

1. Gray
2. Light Violet
3. Violet
4. Light Orange
5. Orange
6. Medium Orange
7. Dark Red
8. Red
9. Blue
10. Light Green
11. Brown
12. Light Brown
13. Light Gray
14. Dark Yellow
15. Light Yellow
16. Yellow
17. Black

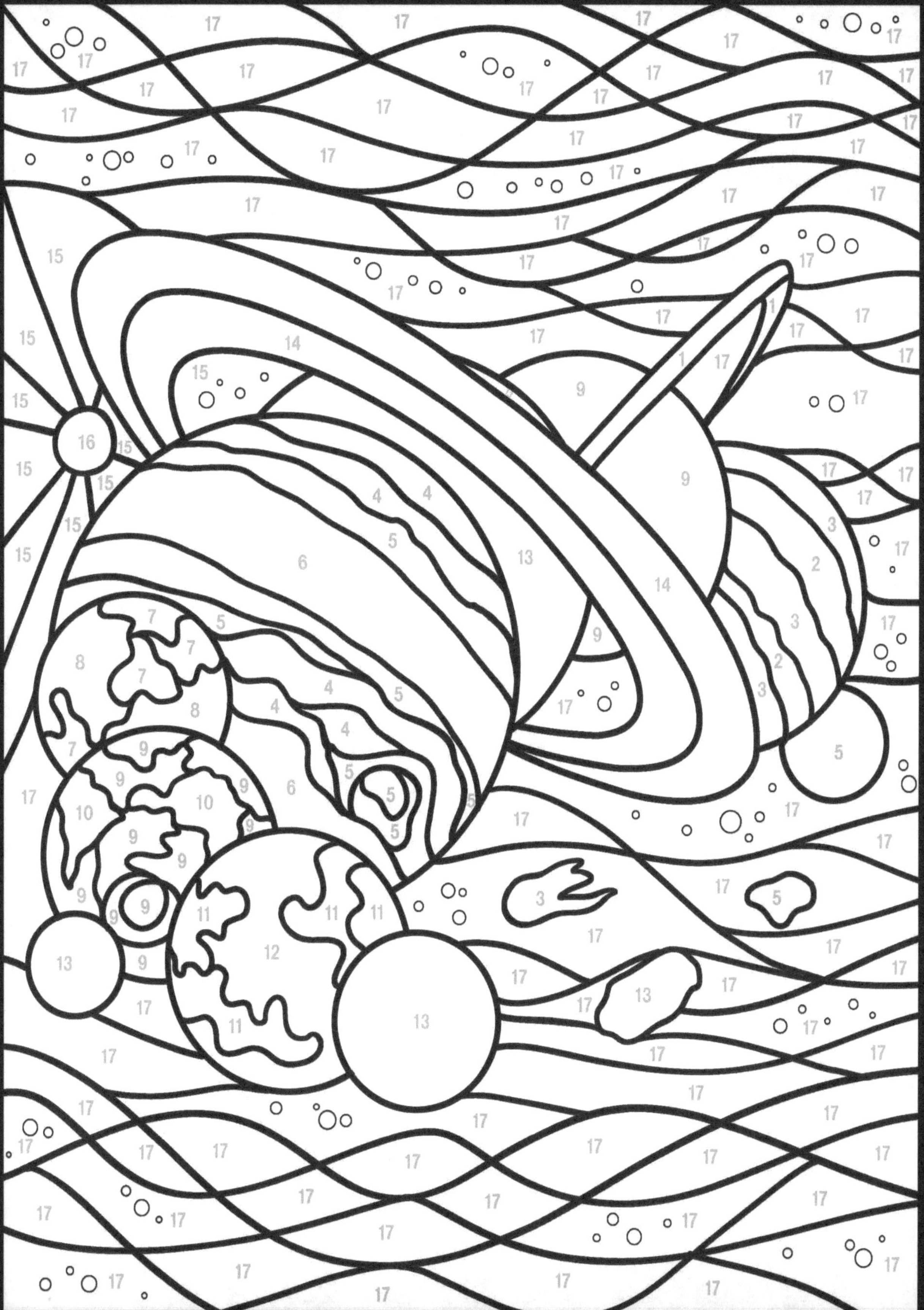

Dragon Fantasy
Mosaic Color By Number
Black Background

1. Black
2. Bright Orange
3. Light Yellow
4. Light Brown
5. Beige
6. Yellow
7. Chocolate
8. Pink
9. Red
10. Brown
11. Medium Brown
12. Dark Brown
13. Medium Orange
14. Bright Orange
15. Light Orange
16. Dark Yellow
17. Soft Violet
18. Baby Blue

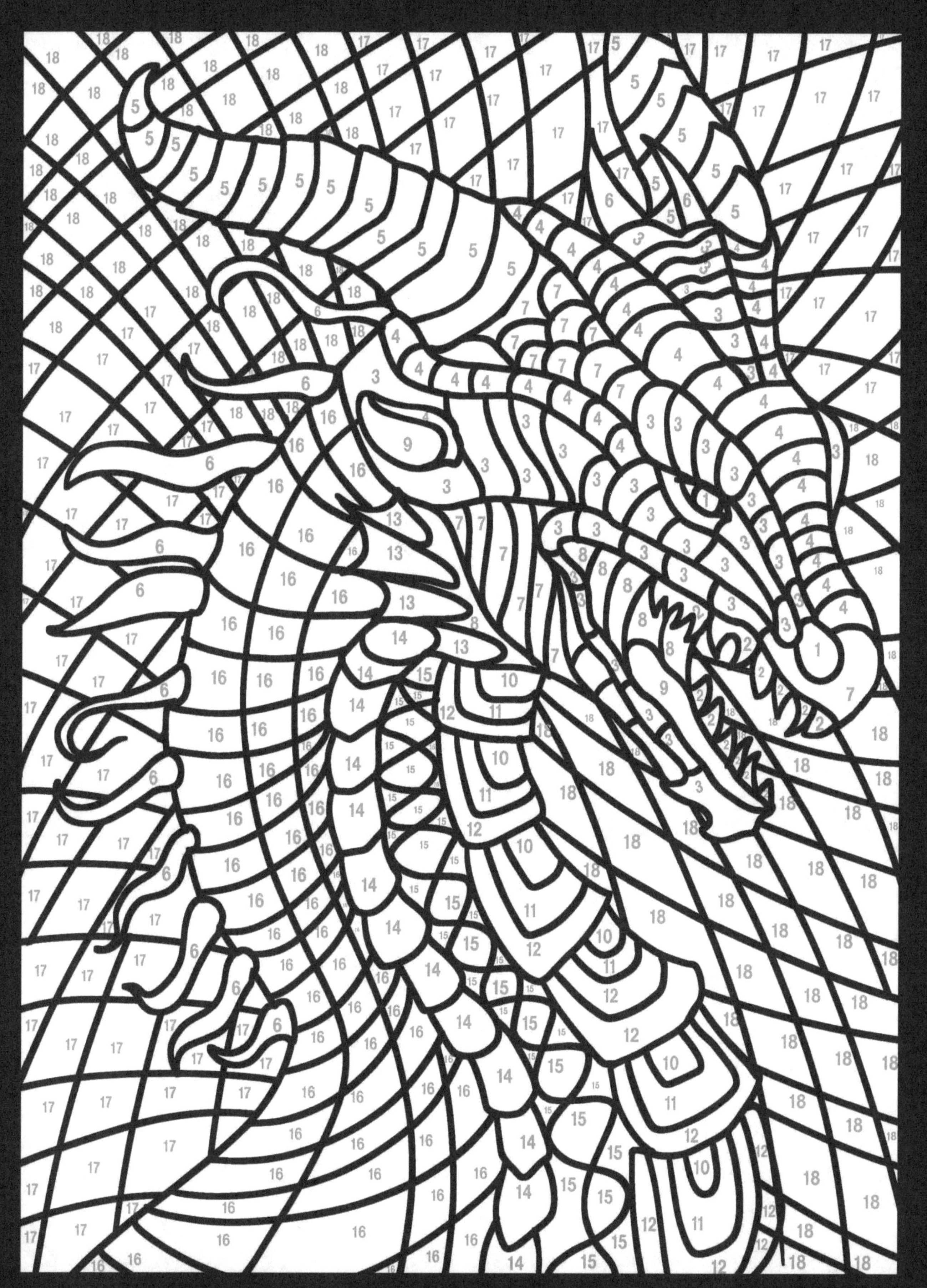

Race Cars, Muscle Cars, Classic Cars
Mosaic Color By Number
BLACK BACKGROUND

1. Black
2. Yellow
3. Light Green
4. Light Orange
5. Dark Orange
6. Dark Gray
7. Orange
8. Blue
9. Light Brown
10. Red
11. Gray
12. Pink
13. Light Violet
14. Light Gray
15. Light Blue
16. Dark Pink
17. Violet

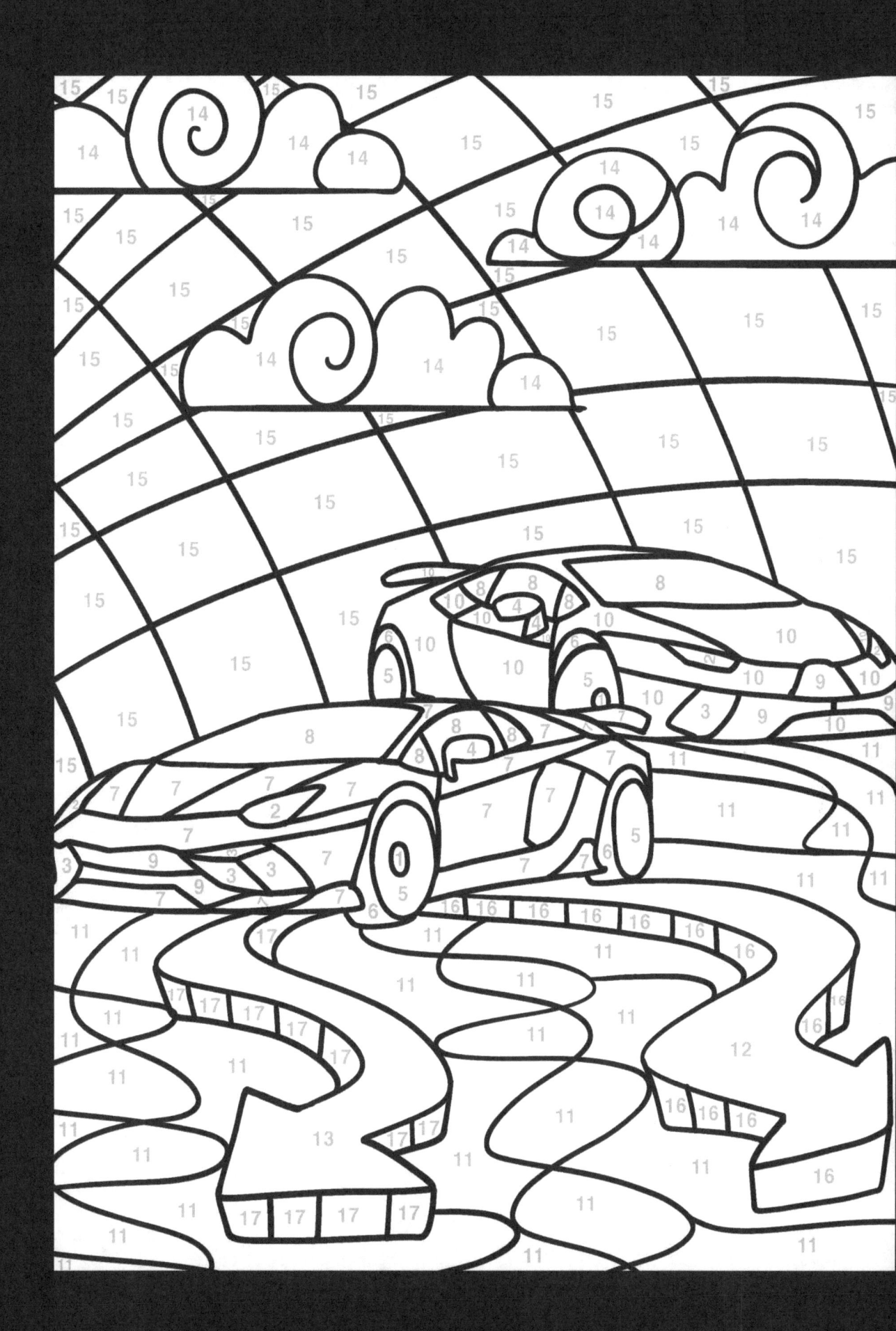

Custom Color Chart

Medium: _ _ _ _ _ _ _ _ _   Brand: _ _ _ _ _ _ _ _ _

1. Black
2. Gray
3. Dark Gray
4. Brown
5. Dark Brown
6. Tan
7. Peach
8. Red
9. Orange Red
10. Orange
11. Light Yellow
12. Yellow
13. Golden Yellow
14. Light Green
15. Green
16. Dark Green
17. Aqua Green
18. Light Blue
19. Blue
20. Dark Blue
21. Lilac
22. Violet
23. Pink
24. Vivid Pink

* Flesh Tone

Custom Color Chart

Medium: _ _ _ _ _ _ _ _ _   Brand: _ _ _ _ _ _ _ _ _

1. _____
2. _____
3. _____
4. _____
5. _____
6. _____
7. _____
8. _____
9. _____
10. _____
11. _____
*12. _____
13. _____
14. _____
15. _____
16. _____
17. _____
18. _____
19. _____
20. _____
21. _____
22. _____
23. _____
24. _____

* _____

Color Testing Sheet

Please Leave Us A Review On Amazon

Made in United States
Troutdale, OR
10/29/2024